This edition published in 1996 by SMITHMARK Publishers, a division of U.S. Media Holdings, Inc., 16 East 32nd Street, New York, NY 10016.

1 2 3 4 5 6 7 8 9

SMITHMARK books are available for bulk purchase for sales promotion and premium use. For details write or call the manager of special sales, SMITHMARK Publishers, 16 East 32nd Street, New York, NY 10016; (212) 532-6600.

ISBN 0-8317-6848-7

CREDITS
Editor: Helen Stone **Design by:** DW Design, London
Color Separation by: Pixel Tech, Singapore
Filmset by: SX Composing Ltd., Essex
Printed in Slovenia

PICTURE CREDITS
Artists
Copyright of the artwork illustrations on the pages following the artists' names is property of Salamander Books Ltd.

Wayne Ford: 7, 26, 31, 53   John Francis: 29
Alan Harris: 32   Guy Troughton: 46

Photographs
The publishers wish to thank the following photographers and agencies who have supplied photographs for this book. The photographs are copyright of the photographer and have been credited by page number and position on the page: (B) bottom or T) top.

Aquila Photographics: M Gilroy; 9, 11, 18, 29, 30, 33, 36, 37, 38, 47, 63
Bruce Colman Ltd.: Jane Burton; 42, 43, Hans Reinhard; 4, 14, 34, 35, 54
Interpet Ltd.: Bernard Bleach; 22 Adrian Turner Photography; 21, 23
Frank Lane Picture Agency Ltd.: A R Hamblin; 20, 25, 49(T), Tony Hamblin; 39, 41, David Hosking; 6, H V Lacey; 4, 49
Cyril Laubscher: title, 8, 10, 12, 13, 17, 44, 50, 56, 57, 61
Jacket photograph © M Gilroy, supplied by Aquila Photographics

Contents

Introduction

Budgies as pets

Colorful and chirpy by nature, the budgerigar is now the most popular pet bird in the world. Millions of these birds are kept in homes, either individually or in groups in an aviary. As companions, their lively chatter and friendliness make them an appealing pet to owners of all ages.

Daily care

Budgies are very easy birds to look after but they do need daily care and attention. You must be prepared to give your budgie fresh food and water every day, and clean out its cage at least three times a week.

Taming and training

Budgies make lively, cheerful companions and develop distinctive characters. The more time you spend training your budgie, the more tame and chatty it will become.

Talkative companions

One of the most famous budgies of all time was called Sparkie Williams. He managed to learn over 500 words. He could also repeat eight whole nursery rhymes and went on to make a recording which sold over 20,000 copies!

General health

Thankfully, well-cared-for budgies are usually healthy pets which rarely fall ill. The average budgie has a lifespan of seven or eight years, but some individuals have been known to live into their twenties.

● *Right:*
The budgie is probably the most popular pet bird. Available in a wide variety of different colors, budgies are easy to tame and develop distinctive personalities.

5

Budgies in the wild

The budgerigar is a member of the parrot family and originally comes from Australia. In their native land, flocks of wild budgies fly across the dry country seeking out seeding grasses and water.

● *Above* and *opposite:* Wild budgies make their homes in the dry interior lands of Australia. They nest in the trees and fly long distances over the dusty landscape looking for food and water.

Feeding grounds

It is not easy to predict where flocks of wild budgies can be seen. They suddenly appear in an area and then may vanish for months if not years, moving on in search of new feeding grounds.

Size and color

Wild budgies are much smaller than their domesticated relatives and are all light green in color, with yellow faces and black barring on their back and wings. Their coloring acts as camouflage and allows them to blend among the trees where they are less likely to be seized by hawks and other hungry predators.

Raising young

Wild budgies nest in tree holes and breed whenever conditions are favorable. This is usually when it rains and new grass is

beginning to grow. By the time the new chicks hatch, there is plenty of seeding grasses to feed them. The new chicks have to learn quickly and after just six weeks, the young budgies are ready to migrate with the adults of the flock to find new food and escape the sweltering heat.

How they got their name

The native Aboriginal people of Australia gave these birds the name *Betcherygah* which roughly translates as "good food". The Aborigines regard young budgie chicks as a delicacy.

Domestication

Budgies first became known outside Australia in the 1770s when skins were taken back to Europe, but it was not until 1840 that the first live budgies reached Europe. They were easy to breed and soon became popular as pets. By the end of the nineteenth century, these birds were being bred in a variety of new colors.

7

Colors of the budgie

There are now thousands of budgie color combinations. Light green is the natural color of wild budgies, although occasionally yellow birds have been recorded among wild flocks. These birds have little hope of survival yet, in an aviary, they thrive and breed without problems.

● *Above:* *The normal Sky Blue budgie and the normal Light Green (opposite, top) are the most common colors of the pet budgerigar.*

Early color changes
Yellow budgerigars were first recorded in Belgium in 1872. Blues followed during the 1880s. Budgerigar fever gripped the world as Japanese buyers paid a fortune for the first white budgies.

The "dark" factor
There are two basic colorations of budgie: the green and the blue. Different shades of these colors are created by the addition of the so-called "dark factor" which darkens the budgie's basic color. In green budgerigars, there is the original shade of Light Green, as well as Dark Green and Olive Green. In blue birds there is the original Sky Blue, Cobalt and Mauve. There are also Violet budgies that are in great demand.

New colors

Gray budgies first appeared in the 1930s and, like blue budgies, can be bred with either white or yellow faces.

Lutinos and Albinos

One of the most popular varieties today is the Lutino which is a rich, buttercup yellow with distinctive red eyes. Albinos are a snowy white color and also have red eyes.

Pieds

Pied budgies have variable areas of yellow and green, or blue and white plumage. The pattern of markings is different on each bird so no two are the same.

Above: The Gray (left), Lutino (center) and Yellow Dominant Pied (right) are popular with pet owners.

● *Left:* The pure white Albino is one of the more unusual colors of budgie.

Wing markings

It is not just the basic color of the budgie which has altered over the last 150 years.

Today's budgies show a wide range of different colored markings on their wings. The classic markings on Light Green budgies are black barring over the wings and three black spots on violet patches across each cheek.

Opalines

One of the first changes to the basic pattern was reported in the early 1930s when the Opaline mutation appeared in Australia and Europe. Opaline budgies have a smaller area of barred patterns at the back of the head and also have a V-shaped area at the top of the wings where there are few or no markings.

● *Above: The normal patterning on the Sky Blue budgie is the same as that of the Light Green, with three black spots and a violet patch on each cheek and black barring over the wings and the back of the head.*
This patterning is reduced in the Opaline budgie (right).

10

Cinnamons, Graywings and Whitewings

During the 1930s the Cinnamon coloring also first appeared. In a Cinnamon budgie, the wing markings and face spots are brown rather than black. In Graywings, the black areas are gray and in Whitewings, these markings are whitish and very pale.

● **Above:** *This Whitewing Violet and the Graywing Sky Blue (opposite) have the typical paler markings of budgies of this type.*

● **Left:** *The Opaline Cinnamon Gray Green has brownish markings in place of the more traditional black.*

11

● **Above:** *These Mauve and Cobalt Spangle budgies have mottled feathers, which create their unusual patterning.*

Spangles

New colors and markings are still appearing even today. One of the most recent is the Spangle, which came from Australia in 1978. A Spangle budgie's body color is normal but the patterns on the wings are changed. This is because each feather is a light color in the center and has a dark edging. Even the throat spots have light centers.

Crests and Tufts

It is not only color that has changed during the budgie's domestication. Different feathering has appeared with the Crested types being most common

12

today. There are three types that can be combined with any budgie pattern or color. The Tufted budgie has a crest which sticks up at the front of its head. The Full-circular Crest has feathers which hang down around the sides of the head. The Half-circular Crest has a similar shape to the Full-circular, but the crest only covers part of the head.

● **Above:** *The Tufted budgie has a crest of feathers on the front of its head.*

Other feather variations

There are also Long-flighted budgies that have long flight feathers so their wings cross over at the back. These birds may have difficulty in flying and are not as popular. There are also rare budgies known as Feather Dusters whose feathers grow unnaturally long. This is more of a defect than a feather type and these birds do not usually live long.

● **Left:** *This Full-crested Gray male has a crest of feathers which hang down the sides of its head.*

Choosing a budgie

If you want a budgie, which will become tame and hopefully learn to talk, start with a youngster aged between six and nine weeks old. At this age, the young bird should already be quite tame and will soon settle into a new home. Older birds will take more time to adjust to new surroundings.

Which color?

There is no link between a budgie's color and its character but if you decide that you want a particular shade, you may have to wait until a suitable chick is available. Some colors are more popular than others and may therefore be more expensive.

Male or female?

When buying a young bird aged between six and nine weeks, it is not always possible to tell whether it is male or female. Once a budgie has molted at four months old the cere, which is the fleshy area above the beak, becomes a more definite color. In a male budgie this is usually blue and in a female it is brown. Chicks of both sexes have a purplish cere.

Singing birds

Cock budgies are often more popular as pets because they have a pretty warbling song. They are also thought to be better mimics than hens, but birds of either sex can be taught to talk without problems.

● **Left:** *There is a wide variety of colors of budgie to choose from.*

Questions *and* Answers

How can I recognize a young budgerigar?
On a young budgie, the wavy pattern of barring on the head goes right down to the cere. The eyes are also completely black without the surrounding white circle seen in adult birds. The cheek spots are smaller and the cere is a purplish color.

Where should I buy my budgie?
If you contact a reputable breeder you may be able to choose a bird while it is still in the nest and you will be certain of its age. Breeders often advertise in local papers, but pet stores also stock a wide selection of young birds.

What should I look for when choosing budgies to breed?
Start with an adult pair of birds which should be at least a year old. If a budgie is wearing a ring around its leg, the year in which it was bred will be printed here.

How can I tell that the budgie I am buying is healthy?
The bird should be lively with smooth feathers, particularly if it is older, and it should be able to fly without difficulty. Its eyes should be clean and bright with no swelling.
Check that the beak is clean and that the upper and lower parts overlap properly. Undershot beaks, where the tip of the upper bill tucks into the lower part, will need to be cut back throughout the budgie's life.
Check that the feet are not gnarled and there are no sores or bleeding.

● **Above:** *The barring on this Cobalt budgie extends right down to its purplish cere, showing that it is a youngster.*

● **Above:** *This adult male budgie has a reduced pattern of barring on its head and white circles around its eyes.*

Understanding your budgie

Budgies are warm-blooded creatures. They keep their temperature stable by panting in hot weather to cool down and by relying on air trapped in their feathers to keep them warm in the cold.

Contour feathers
The two main groups of feathers are known as "flight" and "contour". The budgie's body is covered in small contour feathers which offer protection from the cold and rain.

Flight feathers
The larger feathers at the back of the wings are known as flights These are attached to muscles on the large, light skeleton of the wing. The tail also consists of larger feathers. The budgie will molt from time to time, renewing all of its feathers. In between molts, damaged feathers are preened back into shape.

Eyesight
A budgie's eyesight is much sharper than our own. Because the eyes are on the side of the head, their field of vision is also much wider, allowing them to scan the grasslands for food and would-be predators.

The beak

The budgie's beak is made of a strong, light-weight material, called *keratin*, which is similar to the material which forms our fingernails. Budgies use their beaks for cracking open seeds, preening feathers, and to help them to climb.

● *Above: A budgie uses its beak to help it to climb. If the beak is deformed or undershot, the bird will find it difficult to eat. A cuttlefish is enough to keep an average budgie's beak in trim, but an undershot beak will need to be trimmed back by a vet throughout the budgie's life.*

Housing your budgie indoors

● **Above:** *Cages with both vertical and horizontal bars allow your pet to climb.*

Choosing a cage

Most people keep their budgies in a cage but, if there is room, they can be housed in an indoor flight. Give your budgie as much space as possible and allow it out to fly at a set time each day.

Which design?

Tall, circular cages should be avoided. They provide little flying space. A rectangular design with both vertical and horizontal bars that allow your budgie to climb is much better.

Easy cleaning

It is important to choose a cage which is easy to clean. Ideal designs have either a top which comes away from the base or a sliding draw base. Although silver bars are popular, it is a good idea to choose a cage which is coated with white resin instead. These cages are easier to clean and are less likely to rust.

Securing the doors

Check the door carefully when you are choosing a cage. If the hinge spring becomes weak, your budgie could escape. You can add another clip to the door for safety.

Using a cage stand

A living room is an ideal place for your budgie. The temperature is stable and it can enjoy your company.

Care must be taken with cage stands because they can be knocked over, particularly if you have other pets or very young brothers or sisters. If possible, it is better to stand the cage on a secure table.

Positioning the cage

Check that the cage is not in direct sunlight and there are no drafts which could cause a chill. A light cover can be placed over the cage at night to keep your budgie warm and encourage it to sleep.

● **Above:** *When buying a new cage, it is important to choose one which allows your pet to stay safely inside the cage while you clean it.*

21

Fitting out a cage

Most cages come complete with food dishes, but there are extra fittings that you will need to supply. It is better to provide a separate drinker for water, which can be attached to the bars of the cage. The tubular design keeps the water clean and free of seed husks and droppings.

Cuttlefish and grit
Your budgie will need a cuttlefish bone to keep its beak in trim. This can be attached to the cage with a special clip. If you are using both feeders for seed, you will also need a small pot for grit.

Toys
Toys are popular with most budgies but the cage should not be cluttered with them. A simple mirror above a perch is often appreciated. You may also want a toy which can be fitted onto the perch.

● *Above:* *Don't be tempted to fill your cage with too many toys. Your budgie will appreciate a simple mirror and as much space as possible to move around. Your cage should also be fitted with a cuttlefish to nibble and a separate water drinker (opposite).*

Ladders

Ladders are not a good idea for young budgies because they may get stuck in between the rungs. This is a toy to introduce once your budgie has grown to its full adult size.

Keep it simple

Some budgies enjoy playing with toys that they can roll around the cage floor. A simple table tennis ball is light enough for your budgie to move and easy for you to keep clean.

23

Housing your budgie outdoors

Building a garden aviary is obviously much more expensive than buying a cage but it is practical if you intend to keep a large number of birds. A basic aviary has two parts. An outer flight made of wire netting on a wooden framework and a weatherproof shelter where the birds are fed and can go at night or during bad weather.

Planning and positioning

An aviary should be positioned away from the road in a sheltered part of the garden. The easiest way to build an aviary is to buy a kit which can be put together in the garden on top of a concrete floor. The building should be firmly anchored down on foundations made from bricks or blocks. You may need planning permission to build an aviary.

A safe way in

It is best to have just one door leading into the shelter where the budgies will be fed and watered and an inside door from the shelter to the flight. A safety porch will ensure that no budgies can escape when you enter the aviary.

Fitting out an aviary

As with the cage, an aviary needs to contain a selection of food dishes and water feeders along with toys, such as ladders and swings. Seed hoppers should be placed on a food table inside the shelter along with grit and cuttlefish.

● *Opposite: An aviary makes an ideal home for your budgies if you have a large number of birds. Your pets will enjoy having the company of their own kind and the freedom to fly around. The aviary bird enjoys a lifestyle nearer to that of their wild relatives than a caged budgie kept indoors.*

Cleaning out the cage

Refilling food dishes
At least once a week, the seed dishes should be completely emptied out and washed. It is important to dry seed dishes thoroughly before refilling them or the seed will become damp and turn moldy.

Cleaning water bottles
The water container should also be washed out at least once a week. A bottle brush can be used to clean a tubular drinker, but take care not to force the brush into the base of the drinker because this could split it, causing it to leak.

Keeping the floor clean
The sandsheet in the base of the cage will need to be changed two or three times a week. Store-bought sandsheets that fit the floor of the cage are easy to change, but can be expensive.

Alternative floor linings

Clean, plain paper can be folded to fit the cage and covered with loose bird sand. If you are going to line a cage this way, avoid colored paper or newspaper. Some inks can poison your budgie if it shreds the paper and swallows it.

Base covers

A plastic cover which fits over the base of the cage is useful for keeping the area around the cage clean.

Cleaning fixtures

Once a month, the cage and fittings should be taken apart and cleaned thoroughly using warm water and a disinfectant suitable for birds. Special wipes soaked in pet disinfectant can be bought from pet supply stores and these are safe and simple to use. Toys, perches, and other fittings should be rinsed and dried with a paper towel after cleaning.

● **Above:** *Once a month the cage should be taken apart for thorough cleaning.*

Cleaning an aviary

The food dishes in an aviary should be removed, cleaned, and refilled every day. Hoppers will only need to be refilled as they become half empty. The floor should be swept out daily, and the sleeping quarters should be cleaned of any droppings or food. Once a week, you should wash the floor down and clean any fittings.

27

Questions *and* Answers

How do I prepare a new cage?
It is a good idea to wash a new cage to remove any dust or germs using a disinfectant suitable for birds. This must be rinsed thoroughly before the bird is introduced to the cage. Young budgies are most likely to fall ill, so it is especially important to put them in clean surroundings.

What are the best type of perches?
Plastic or doweling perches tend to be a standard thickness and so it is a good idea to add other branches so your budgie doesn't get sore feet. Extra perches can be cut from apple trees which have not been sprayed and should be washed in case they have been soiled by wild birds. If your cage has end caps to hold the perch in place, ask an adult to trim the ends of the branch to fit.

Where should I place perches in an aviary?
The sleeping area of an aviary needs several perches at roughly the same height so there is no jostling for the best position. It is also good to place perches in part of the flight where rain will fall to allow your budgies to shower.

Where is the best place to position the cage?
Although budgies come from a warm climate, they do not like bright sun. Never place a cage directly in front of a window or your budgie may get heat stroke, which can be fatal. Next to a wall, in a bright corner of the room is the best place. Position the cage at eye-level to make it easier to see and tame your new budgie.

● **Above:** *Perches cut from tree branches are a good alternative to plastic or doweling perches which are a standard thickness. Gripping the same thickness of perch can give your budgie sore feet after a while.*

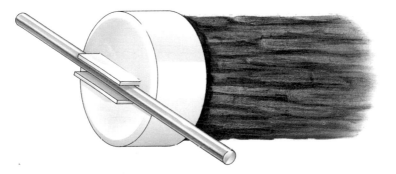

● **Above:** *Branches can be used to replace the doweling perches in your budgie's cage. Many perches are fitted with end caps which clip onto the bars at the side of the cage. The new branch can be trimmed to fit the existing end caps.*

Feeding your budgie

Budgies eat mostly seed and it is easy to provide
them with a suitable diet. Budgerigar seed mixtures
bought from pet stores contain millet, which are the
round seeds and canary seeds, which are oval-
shaped. Some seed mixtures have added vitamins
and minerals, which is better than ordinary seed.
Budgies only eat the kernel inside the seed and you
will see the empty husks in and around the food dish.

● *Above: Along with seed, fresh foods should also form an
important part of your budgie's diet. Always wash fresh
foods thoroughly to remove any harmful chemicals.*

Refilling the food dish

Fresh seed should be added to the seed dish each
day. The dish does not need to be completely
emptied each time, but can be shaken to bring empty
husks to the surface. These should be brushed off
before new seed is added on top.

Additional treats

Budgies also like millet sprays, which can be fixed
near a perch using a peg, but it is not good to let
your budgie eat millet spray as its main food. You
can also buy seed treats for your pet. Some brightly
colored treats may turn your budgie's droppings an
odd color. It is important to bear this in mind or you
may think your pet is ill.

Extra vitamins

Some budgies may need extra vitamins and minerals
and can be given a special supplement which is sold
in pet shops. Always read the instructions carefully,
as too much could be harmful.

Fresh food

Fresh foods should also form part of your budgie's
diet. Greens such as chickweed, dandelion, and
seeding grasses, as well as carrots and apples can be
given, but these should be washed first to remove
any harmful chemicals.

● **Above:** *Suitable foods include: 1. millet spray 2. seed
treats 3. seed mixture 4. fresh food 5. grit 6. cuttlefish.*

Grooming and handling

It is important to be able to catch and handle your budgie properly without hurting it. Watch how the person who sells you the budgie catches the bird. If you are right-handed, reach this hand into the cage and place it over the budgie either when it is on the perch or after it flutters to the floor.

Handling your budgie

Gently wrap your fingers around the sides of the body and gradually adjust your grip so that the bird's head rests between your first and second fingers with its back lying in the palm of your hand. It is very important not to put any pressure on the sides of the budgie's neck because this will make it difficult for it to breathe.

● *Above: This is the correct way to hold a budgie. Its wings and back are supported in the palm of the hand and the head is facing forward. In this position, it is difficult for the budgie to bite.*

Checking condition

When held in this way, the budgie shouldn't struggle, nor will it be able to bite you. You will be able to examine most of its body, beak, and feet. Check to see if it has lost weight by feeling for the breastbone running down the center of the body from the lower chest downward. This should be well-covered by muscle on either side.

● ***Above:*** *A budgie bath can be introduced into the cage on a warm day to help keep your budgie's feathers in good condition. Many budgies enjoy splashing around in water.*

Bath time

A budgie kept indoors will not have the opportunity to bathe when it rains and so its feathers can become dry and ruffled. Budgie baths are available. These fit over the cage door, but not all budgies enjoy bathing in still water.

You can spray your pet instead, using one of the fine mist sprayers sold for plants. Fill this with lukewarm water and, having removed the food dishes, gently spray just above the bird's head so that the water droplets fall like rain.

33

Taming your budgie

The time you spend talking to and playing with your new budgie will encourage the bird to become tame. Budgies are sociable by nature and enjoy company, so if you are keeping just one bird, it is important that you spend time with it every day.

When it comes to training, you need to be patient. Short teaching sessions of 10-15 minutes give the best results and you can try two or three sessions a day. You can start training once your budgie has settled in with you.

Finger training

The first step in training is to teach your budgie to perch on your finger. Slowly place your hand in the cage, taking care not to frighten the bird, and extend your index (first) finger alongside the perch. Move your finger up to touch the budgie's toes to encourage it to step onto your finger from the perch. At first the bird may fly to another perch or down to the floor, but it shouldn't be long before it is happily sitting on your finger.

Letting your budgie out of its cage

When your budgie is confident about sitting on your finger, the next stage is to encourage your pet to stay on your hand as you move it toward the door of the cage. Before actually allowing the bird to come out of the cage, you must make sure that there are no hazards in the room which could harm your budgie (see *Making the room safe, page 38*).

● *Opposite* and *Below:*
Budgies that are handled regularly will become tame and hopefully learn to talk.

Teaching tricks and learning to talk

Feeding from your hand
When your budgie is used to being handled, you may be able to train it to eat from your hand. Start by first offering a favorite food through the side of the cage and then encourage your pet to take the tidbit directly from your hand. You may also be able to teach your pet to play with toys on command. Setting the toy in motion while giving a verbal command such as "swing" will give your pet a clear idea of what the command means.

Learning to talk

Budgies best learn to talk if taught by just one person. They respond well to a woman's or child's voice. When teaching your pet to talk, the room must be quiet. Too many people crowding around or a radio playing in the background may confuse your budgie and make it hard for it to concentrate.

Introducing new phrases

Start with a simple phrase such as "good morning" or your budgie's name. Repeat the phrase regularly and always in exactly the same way. Changing the

words or the way in which you say them will confuse your pet. Before long, your budgie will be mimicking the words and you can move on to new phrases. Be patient. If you rush the lessons, the budgie will become muddled and start repeating words in the wrong order.

Some budgies never talk, but with patience even reluctant talkers can usually be taught to whistle tunes.

● *Left: Budgies are attentive pets, capable of learning tricks. Training sessions should be frequent and kept short otherwise your budgie will become confused or may lose interest.*

Making the room safe

Most budgies welcome time out of their cage to exercise but, before you let your budgie out into the room, you must make sure that the room is safe.

Closed windows

Windows are one of the biggest hazards. A budgie may not see the glass and attempt to fly straight through it. Sadly, this kind of accident usually proves fatal, but can be avoided by covering the windows with net curtains.

Open doors and windows

You must also make sure that all the windows and doors are closed. Tell other people in the home that your budgie is flying in the room, otherwise they may open the door and allow the bird to fly out.

Contact with other pets

You must keep other pets, particularly cats, out of the room. Aquariums and fishtanks should be covered. The bird could fall in and drown. Budgies can also become ill by drinking fishtank water.

Fires and fans

Open fires are very dangerous and must be completely screened off before the budgie is allowed out of the cage. Heaters and fans should be switched off in advance and any ornaments that could be knocked over should be put away. Remove any plants which might be poisonous if your budgie ate them.

Regular exercise

When first let out of the cage, your budgie will probably fly around wildly but eventually, it should come to rest on its cage. Try to allow your pet out to exercise once a day to keep it fit and happy.

● *Below:* *Your budgie will enjoy spending time out of its cage, but you must be careful to remove any dangers such as houseplants which may be poisonous if eaten (opposite).*

Questions *and* Answers

Are there are any foods which I should not feed my budgie?
It is not a good idea to feed your budgie avocado which is likely to be poisonous. Also avoid salty foods and those containing a lot of fat. Peas are quite safe and some budgies even like dried fruits, such as raisins. Never feed your budgie kitchen scraps or sweets. These are not suitable foods and can only harm your pet.

Why do budgies need grit?
Like other birds, budgies have no teeth and so they use grit in their gizzard to break down the seeds they have eaten. You can buy special grit for budgies from pet supply stores. Replace the contents of the grit dish every two weeks. This way there will always be different-sized particles of grit available to your budgie.

Do budgies need both cuttlefish bones and iodine blocks?
These provide two vital minerals and should be available to budgies at all times. Cuttlefish bone supplies calcium, which is necessary for a healthy skeleton and muscles, as well as being the major ingredient of eggshells. Iodine is used for making chemical messengers, called hormones, which are important for the molting process. Bird seed doesn't contain enough calcium or iodine, which is why these extra things are necessary.

How should I store food?
Food should be bought in small amounts to ensure that it is always fresh. Once the package is opened, loose seed should be stored in a clean,

dry, airtight container. Always use all the food in the container before adding a new batch.

I keep trying to teach one of my aviary budgies to talk, but I don't seem to be getting anywhere. Why is this?

Budgies are sociable birds which live in flocks in the wild. When no other company is available, they look to their owner for communication and this is how they learn to talk. When there are plenty of other birds around, they use their own natural language and are unlikely to respond to your attempts to teach them human phrases.

● *Below: A cuttlefish helps to keep a budgie's beak in trim and provides necessary calcium.*

Budgie behavior

When you first get your budgie, you may find that it spends a lot of time on the floor of its cage. This is because chicks aren't used to perching for long periods of time. But do keep a close watch on your new pet, because this can also be a sign of illness. The young budgie should hop up onto the perch when you approach its cage.

● *Above:* *This Sky Blue cock is feeding an Albino hen, showing typical courtship behavior.*

Display behavior

As a cock budgie becomes older, it will begin to sing more. You may also see him tap at the perch with his beak while singing. At the same time, his eyes may appear to become whiter for a brief period. This is typical budgie display behavior.

The cere of a hen becomes a deep shade of brown when she is ready to breed and she may also nibble more determinedly at the cuttlefish bone. The cuttlefish is a valuable source of calcium which the hen's body needs to make eggshells.

Budgerigars' sociable nature may become more noticeable during the breeding season. A pair of budgies may feed each other and the cock will often preen his mate.

Molting

There will be times of the year, however, when your budgie is quieter than normal. This is usually linked to the molting period, when the budgie grows a new set of feathers. The old feathers will fall out over a couple of months as the new plumage replaces them.

The older budgie

As they grow older, hens may become more destructive and shred sandsheets in the bottom of their cage. This is nesting behavior and the hen may even lay eggs. Cocks are more likely to feed either mirrors or toys on their cage.

● *Right: These cock budgies are showing mild aggression by trying to out-stare each other.*

Introducing a second budgie

Having had a pet budgie for a time, you may decide that you want to get a companion for your bird or even start breeding them. Although they are sociable by nature, not all budgies appreciate the sudden introduction of another bird to their cage. Introductions should be carried out carefully to avoid distress and fighting.

● **Above:** *A new budgie must be introduced gradually to your existing pet. It may be some weeks before you can house them in the same cage.*

Treating a new bird

A new bird should be kept in a second cage for a couple of weeks to make sure that it is healthy and to help it to adjust to its new surroundings. The new budgie should be treated with spray to kill any mites or feather lice. This is available from a pet supply store or your vet. Follow the instructions on the label and repeat as necessary until you are certain that your new budgie is completely free of bugs.

Making contact

Keep the budgies within sight and sound of each other after the first week. This will give them a chance to get to know each other from a distance. If you are planning to breed them, introduce them into the breeding cage at the same time so that the environment will be new to both of them.

Changing behavior

If your original budgie is already talking, it may stop and revert back to its natural language when placed with another bird. With perseverance, you should find that the bird continues to talk. On rare occasions, a good talking budgerigar may even encourage its new companion to speak.

Breeding budgies

Although budgies housed indoors and in aviaries may start nesting at any time of year, it is better to limit breeding to the spring and summer.

Pairing birds

As the breeding period approaches, the hen's cere will become deep brown and she will become very confidant. Both male and females may also start to regurgitate food. Budgies choose their own mates, but it is important to make sure that there are no unpaired birds left in an aviary because this will cause fighting. You need to provide about twice as many nest boxes as pairs, in the covered part of the aviary at the same height. This will stop any squabbling over individual nesting sites.

Providing a nest box

If you have one pair of budgies, they can be moved to a special breeding cage fitted with a nest box. Inside the nest box, there is a removable wooden base with a hollowed center where the hen will lay her eggs. This is called a *concave*. A pane of glass or perspex behind the opening allows you to look into the box without any risk of the birds flying out.

Always tap on the outside first to let your budgies know that you are opening their nest box. When the hen is ready to lay, she will spend more time in the nest box and her droppings will become larger.

● **Above:** *Breeding budgies will need to be provided with a nest box (opposite). A single nest box can be attached to a breeding cage if you have just one pair of birds.*

Laying eggs

The hen will lay white eggs on alternate days, producing five or six in an average clutch. She will incubate them on her own until each egg hatches about 18 days after it was laid.

Feeding nesting birds

When the chicks hatch, they are blind and helpless but they grow very quickly. The adult birds feeding the chicks should be fed a special rearing food to help them cope with their hungry family and you may need to provide a second drinker of water.

Cleaning the nest box

It is very important to keep the nest box clean. Wash the food dishes every day using a detergent and rinse them thoroughly with clean water. The concave in the nest box will also need changing as the chicks grow older, but this should not be done before the chicks are two weeks old.

Move the chicks to a clean, empty plastic container or a similar box while you change the concave. The dirty one should be soaked in a bucket of water and then scrubbed clean and left to dry.

Caring for new chicks

You must handle new chicks very carefully. Their claws may become caked in dirt and this should be removed by holding the chick's foot in a container of lukewarm water. When the dirt is soft, it can be gently broken off, taking care not to harm the chick's claws.

You should also check the beak to see that there is no dirt inside. This

could cause the bill to grow out of shape. Any dirt can be gently scraped away with a blunt toothpick or the plain end of a dead match.

● **Above:** *These four-day old chicks are completely helpless, but in just a few weeks they will be growing their first feathers (below), and will be ready to leave the nest at six weeks old.*

The growing chick

Before the chicks grow their first feathers, they will first develop a coat of grayish-white down. You should see the first feathers by the time the young budgies are about three weeks old and by five weeks they should be fully feathered. At this stage, the young birds will be ready to leave the nest.

Leaving the nest
The cock bird will feed the older chicks until they can eat on their own at about six weeks old. By the time the chicks leave the nest box, the mother hen may have laid another clutch of eggs.

Returning to the nest
If the first chicks insist on returning to the nest box, they could soil the new eggs with their droppings. This may stop the eggs from hatching, so it is important to move the young budgerigars to another cage as soon as you are sure they can feed themselves.

Feeding the young
Young budgies should be fed a mixture of regular seed and the rearing food you offered the adult birds. The protein in this food will help the young budgies grow and, in due course, they will be used to this food when they have chicks of their own.

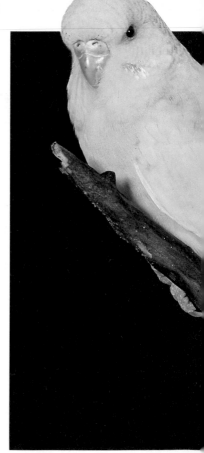

How many chicks?

Budgies should not be allowed to have more than two rounds of chicks without a break. To stop them breeding, the birds should go back to their flights and nest boxes should be removed from the aviary.

Separating males and females

Once the young budgies start to molt at 12 weeks, you should separate the males and females. If the chicks are going to new homes, this is the ideal age for them to go as they will settle better while young.

● **Below:** *These young budgies are at the ideal age to tame and are ready to go to their new homes.*

Mixing with other pets

It is not generally a good idea to allow budgies to mix with other pets, particularly cats, which are their natural enemies. If you already have a cat, then you will need to keep a close eye on it to see that it does not disturb your budgie. You should position the bird's cage in part of the room that will be hard for the cat to reach.

Cats
At first, the budgie is likely to get distressed and fly around wildly whenever it sees the cat. Of course, all this activity is likely to attract the attention of the cat to the bird. In time, the cat will come to realise that it cannot reach the budgie and the bird will accept that it is not in immediate danger from the cat and the two will no longer bother each other. Even so, never be tempted to risk leaving the cat alone with the budgie.

Dogs
Dogs rarely resent the addition of a bird to your home and are not likely to cause any trouble while your bird is safely in its cage. However, it is not a good idea to let the budgie out of the cage while your dog is in the room.

Other birds
If you already have other birds, particularly larger parrots, you will also need to be careful as they can be surprisingly spiteful to a smaller bird. For the same reason, it is not a good idea to house your budgie with a smaller bird which could in turn be bullied. Never allow your budgie out if there is a larger parrot in the room. Cockatiels are usually more gentle and can be allowed to mix with your budgie but, they shouldn't be left alone. Cages housing parrots and budgies should be placed far apart, so there is no risk of the parrot being able to injure the budgie through the sides of the cage.

Guinea pigs and rabbits

Although some people keep guinea pigs or rabbits on the floor of an aviary housing budgies, it is probably better to keep them apart so there is no danger of passing on diseases.

● **Above:** *The cat is a budgie's natural enemy and the two should never be left alone.*

Going on vacation

When going away, it is important to arrange for your budgie to be looked after as early as possible. If you have an aviary of birds and belong to a local bird club, you may be able to arrange with a fellow member to look after each other's budgies during vacations. Some boarding kennels also cater for smaller pets, such as budgerigars. Be sure to find out whether you should provide food, or simply pay for this on your return.

Providing a care list
Write out a list of what your pet eats, along with its age and the name, address, and telephone number of your vet, in case the bird gets sick while you're away.

Taking your budgie on vacation
If you are going away with a large trailer or caravan or staying in a rented cottage, you may be able to take your pet with you. Never leave your budgie in the car. The temperature in a locked vehicle can rise to a fatal level in just minutes. Make sure that the cage is secure and there is no risk of the budgie escaping.

● *Right: It is not usually difficult to find someone to care for your budgie while you are on vacation. Your pet can be taken to its temporary home in its cage.*

CHECKLIST – Going on vacation

- Arrange for someone to look after your pet in advance.
- Provide sufficient food and supplies.
- Write a list of daily care and feeding instructions.
- Leave the name and number of your vet.

The first signs of illness

One of the most obvious signs of illness in budgies to watch for is a change in the appearance of the droppings. Typically, these turn green if the bird loses its appetite or suffers from a digestive disorder. Other signs to look for are breathing difficulties, dull or swollen eyes, or ruffled feathers. There may be crusting around the eyes and cere. This usually indicates a disease caused by tiny mites called *scaly face*, which can be treated easily. A sick bird may look sleepy and lose interest in its toys and you, preferring to sit in a hunched fashion on its perch.

Seeking advice

It is important to see a vet as soon as a budgie shows the first sign of being ill because its condition may worsen very quickly. The food dish can alert you to sickness quite early on. The dark kernels of the canary seed which the bird has cracked but not eaten, along with the fluffed-up appearance of your budgie suggest that it has a problem affecting its digestive tract. Unfortunately, the symptoms of many bird illnesses are very similar which is why it is important to get professional help. A vet will be able to run tests and provide antibiotics, which can help to save the life of a sick bird.

● *Opposite: A budgie sitting hunched on its perch and showing no interest in its surroundings is obviously sick and in need of attention. A vet may keep your budgie for observation until the illness can be diagnosed (above).*

Going to the vet

When taking your budgie to the vet, you should carry the bird in a secure cardboard box with air holes punched in the side, rather than in its cage. Birds are generally less upset when traveling in a closed container in semidarkness instead of an open cage.

CARE CHECKLIST

DAILY

What to do Add new seed, brushing away any old seed husks first.

Provide fresh water.

Remove any left over fresh food from the previous day.

Provide fresh fruit, greens, and vegetables.

What to look for Check that the seed has been eaten.

Check that there are no leaks or blockages in the drinker.

WEEKLY

What to do Remove the tray at the bottom of the cage and replace the lining about two or three times each week.

Wash out the drinker.

Scrub and roughen the perches if necessary or replace them.

Check supplies of seed and other items.

Spray your budgie with water from a plant sprayer before cleaning out the cage.

Empty the cover around the base of the cage.

Clean the aviary floor and check the sleeping quarters.

What to look for Look for any change in the budgie's droppings, which could indicate a health problem.

Check for any damage to the cage or aviary structure and fittings.

Check for signs of rats or mice around the aviary outside.

MONTHLY

What to do Strip down the cage and wash it thoroughly.

Wash the cage cover if the budgie is being covered at night with a towel.

What to look for Check that your budgie's claws are not overgrown and arrange trimming if necessary.

Check that the door of the cage is secure.

Check the weatherproofing of the aviary.

Questions *and* Answers

Do I need to have my budgie's claws trimmed regularly?
This may be necessary if the claws grow at an odd angle, or curl around making it difficult for your budgie to climb around in its cage.
Arrange for your vet to trim the bird's claws. A proper pair of bone clippers should be used, rather than scissors, which will split the claws.

What is the major cause of death in budgies?
A common problem in older budgies is different types of tumors. Watch for swellings on the body, particularly around the breastbone. They are called *lipomas* and can become quite large, making it difficult for the budgie to fly. Lipomas can be removed by surgery, which will help the budgie to continue flying without problems. Unfortunately, lipomas do sometimes grow back. A noticeable change in the budgie's cere color, along with weight loss may be a symptom of an internal tumor. The kidneys and sex organs are often affected and treatment in these cases is, sadly, impossible.

How can I tell if my budgie has breathing problems\?
The first sign is usually a gentle wheezing. Keep your budgie warm and keep a close eye on it until you can contact a vet for advice.
More advanced symptoms include a general weakness and hunched position, heavy breathing through an open beak, and a jerking action of the tail. In this case, you should seek medical help immediately.

What is the cause of scaly face?
Scaly face is caused by parasites which are
found around the beak and sometimes on the
legs. An early sign of the disease is small snail-
like tracks across the bill which may spread to
form small crusty lumps around the side of the
beak. This condition can be treated quite easily,
but if it is left untreated it may cause permanent
damage to the beak.

*My budgie's feathers are ruffled and there
are feathers at the bottom of the cage. I am
worried that she is sick.*
It sounds as though your budgie is molting,
which is a completely normal process. Your
budgie may be quieter during this time but if
she shows other symptoms you should contact
your vet for advice.

● *Above: Budgies may need to have their claws trimmed
from time to time, especially if they grow very long or at a
strange angle. A vet will be able to trim the claws, avoiding
the blood supply. This should be painless for your pet.*

About my budgie

MY BUDGIE'S NAME IS

Darell

MY BUDGIE'S BIRTHDAY IS

July 15

Stick a photo of your budgie here

THE COLOR OF MY BUDGIE IS

yellow and green

MY BUDGIE'S FAVORITE FOOD IS

Peect food

MY BUDGIE'S FAVORITE PHRASE IS

I love you!

MY VET'S NAME IS

MY VET'S TELEPHONE NUMBER IS

Index